Songs from the Heart

By

Barbara Carter

authorHOUSE

1663 LIBERTY DRIVE, SUITE 200
BLOOMINGTON, INDIANA 47403
(800) 839-8640
www.authorhouse.com

AuthorHouse™
1663 Liberty Drive, Suite 200
Bloomington, IN 47403
www.authorhouse.com
Phone: 1-800-839-8640

AuthorHouse™ UK Ltd.
500 Avebury Boulevard
Central Milton Keynes, MK9 2BE
www.authorhouse.co.uk
Phone: 08001974150

First published by AuthorHouse 2/14/2006

ISBN: 1-4184-0966-9 (e)
ISBN: 1-4184-0967-7 (sc)

Printed in the United States of America
Bloomington, Indiana

This book is printed on acid-free paper.

Ms Carter had her first poem Hear Me published in 1995. She currently resides in Gaines Townships. She's a mother of two children and a Grandmother of two. Other outside activities include computers, web design and family.

Hear Me!

I whom was made from the rib of man
Have struggled hard, just to be by your side
Only to find that I have fallen short
of what I cherish the most…
my child, my man, my family.

Hear me, Black man!
I speak from my soul, from deep within my heart
From my lips, to your ears,
Oh! Hear me black man, for I am yours

We have traveled, so far together
To let it end now
Look back, to where we were and what we were
A Strong, Black, United family.

Now go my black man and grow strong
As you were meant to be
A beautiful strong black man
For the future, is truly in your hands.

Grasp the star that shines so bright,
Then pull us close by your side
And never ever let us go.

Barbara Carter

Tuskegee Airmen

Tuskegee Airmen flying high
Black men flying by your side
From left to right, they fly with pride
332nd, Black airmen of the sky

Mission to mission, they fly on by
You know they'll bring you back alive
No recognition of what they do
But they die fighting to keep you alive

And those that survive,
To returned with pride
Are hit with reality,
They are still at the end of the line

Though we owe them our future
From our past they have died
Tuskegee Black Airmen
We owe you our lives.

Freedom

My dream is freedom
That when I lay down
And close my eyes
I shall be free

Free like the birds,
that fly over the heavenly sky
We are the children, that must survive

My dream, my dream is freedom
That one day, we shall be free
free to walk, free to talk
free to be whomever we may choose

We are the children of tomorrow
we will survive
My dream, my dream,
My dream is Freedom.

Savage

You call me a savage
Not worthy of thee
But, was it not you
Who bought us to be
To this land
That is far and foreign to me

But yet you call me
A savage in heat
When it is you, who knocks,
Not to speak.

You who have mate us,
Enslaved us then sell us
Now this I ask!
Who is the savage?
surely not I.

Brother

The thought, of losing you,
Was much greater than I
It overwhelmed me
With pain and sorrow,
the day that you die.

Oh! Brother of mine,
Where are you right now?
I know in my mind
Where you have gone,
But my heart aches out
for that brother of mine.

They say rest in peace
And I know that you are,
But how do I move on
From this day until' the end of my time

I love you, I miss you,
Dear brother of mine.
I know in the end
Together we'll be
From that day on
until eternity.

Prejudice

If one could only look beyond
Their own prejudice
From which they are bound

Then they would see that
we who are hurting
Are hurting ourselves

Bonded by prejudice
We are all brothers and sisters
who desires the same

But if one could only look
Beyond our own prejudice
From which they are bound.

A Friend

A woman who is meant to be
my friend, my lady
my forever loving wife

I can't began to tell you
What I really need
for everything in this world
has always been you

From the day I was born
'till the day I die
I know the mother I had, is within you

I would kiss away the sorrows
the bed time blues
just to see a smile come over you

So forgive me, my love
for the neglect and pain
because within you, I have not only a wife
but a life long friend.

Forgiveness

There's no forgiveness to be given
For the love we have
is strong enough to carry us through
All I ask is that you learn
from the mistakes we have made
so we may grow stronger together

I know the man and woman we are
is strong enough to over come any
and all short comings in our lives

You're the one I have chosen
to share my life for an eternity.
You're everything good
and nothing, that I can fear

So there's no forgiveness to be given
For the love we have
is strong enough to carry us through

Bring Me Inside

When we come together
We seem to explode
There's no other joy
I care to know

From dusk to dawn
and early on
There's no substitute
For your sweet charm

So delight me my darling
With your tender lips
My heart beats louder
With your every touch

Now caress me my darling
And come inside
There's no other warmth
I care to find

My Child's Eyes

When I look in my child's eyes
I see a since of loss
what's wrong I ask
with no response

I have given all I had to give
hoping she'd grow to be
more than I

But when I look in my child's eyes
I see a great fear
worse than mine

I can only love her and hold her
but I can take away that fear
In those beautiful brown eyes

Oh...God!
where have I gone wrong
In my child's eyes

Beauty in My Eyes

My beautiful black woman
by my side you stand unique
but, yet alone you are strong
you are a pillar of strength in my eyes

When I look at your black beauty
it excels above all
you are a goddess in my eyes

I can only cherish what you are
a woman to be admired
never to be pity
You are a true vision of beauty in my eyes

Oh! no one knows as well as I
what you have and will endeavor
But yet your strong and you still move on

With just a touch of Africa within your soul
you arise above the rest
You are truly, a beauty in any mans my eyes

For there's no award to be given
But here by my side come beauty of my eyes
take your throne by my side
A Beauty in my eyes

We the People

We the people have changed
We are no longer the strong
We are no longer the loving people
We are no longer God's chosen ones
We have become what we once feared
We are them

Unknown Culture

You have join us together
so you may fear not, what you fear the most
a people strong living free in a world
of culture unknown to your own

Surviving in a time once known
and forgotten by your world
people working together as one

How could this be
civilization in a world so primitive to mine
working together
to have for the have knots

Who am I?

Who am I
can I truly answer this question

I am not white
for my skin is too dark
I am not African
for I can not speak their language
I am not Indian
nor do I speak their language

So, who am I?
I am an American
I am the progeny of you all

Mahogany

From the open wide lands of Africa
to the shackles on my feet
I of, Mahogany skin
Has risen to every occasion

With my curly black hair
My big brown eyes
My luscious lips
And my bodacious body

Who am I!
I am Goddess
Your blood flows through my veins
So I am worthy to wear this crown
now and for ever .

Life will never change

I can't feel pass the pain
it seems as though my life will never change
new faces, new places,
yet everything stays the same

I must be wearing a sign
hurt me, will you please
I can't feel alive right now
for something keeps me hurting
deep down inside

50 Years of Blessings

God must have bless the day
You both found one another
I have never seen you both look so in love
On your 50th year

It's a treasure to see
the gift of Love
Flowing so gracefully

If I should be so lucky
To have the love you share
Then I will know that God has shined
his blessings down on me

Barbara Carter

Questions of Love

Love, what's it all about
Is it do as I say not as I do
Is it I'm before you and you after me
Is it help me, help me, help me please
Is it gimme, gimme, gimme my needs
Is it take care of me then take care of you
Is it a lover who's only on call
Is it a mate who still goes on dates
Is it the one who's never here for me
Is it the money from my hands to yours
Or is it a friend you can always depend on
I thought I once knew what it's all about
But, what is love does anybody really know???

How do I Survive

A lost soul wondering around in place
not knowing where to go
when it will all end
how will I survive
here all alone on my own.

Confused out of place
I'm at a lost of words
with no place to call home

Is this it is this the end
who will I love who will care for me
how do I survive
here all alone

A Familiar Face

Around the corner through the door
Sleek tall built over my head
Beyond my reach came
A familiar face
But yet a stranger from the past
Someone I had never knew

Our path crossing over but yet again
Softly speaking our hello's
Conversations of the past
No real meaning we move on
But yet we are drawn by our past

this strange encounter of what's in common
For this dear friend will last
for how much longer?

Thinking of you

Sometimes I think of you
Sometimes I smile too
But sometimes there's no room
For the pain I feel inside

Reaching out in every direction
But yet fearing what's in this for me
This strange but, delightful person
Confuses but so

I'm charmed by his words
Overwhelmed by his touch
But yet afraid of what's to come

A trusting life, I don't know
The unknown fears me so
He's someone I want to love
He's someone I care for

But when I think of you
I think of how our love has grown
But when I think beyond this time
these feelings cease to grow.

Sunshine and Water

You say a mans home is his castle
to rule over and to give guidance
to give and receive respect
to show love and affection

This is your power of control
you are the controlling factor of your young
like flowers need sunshine and water to grow
or it would die never reaching full growth

So shall the child whose misguided parents
has left him to survive all on his own

A flower needs sunshine and water to grow
a child needs both parents in order to know
which way to go to grow up right

A father is the sunshine that strengthens a child
but for a girl he's the role model, of a good mate
with the directions of a life for which she will take

A mother is the water that natures a child
but, for a boy she teaches feelings, love, compassion
and the understanding of a woman

So remember this if nothing at all
A child ask not to be born
this act of life you have taken upon yourself
Now until you see what you must do
these young lives shall never know
these young innocent lives
will never survive

Men

Where have all the real men gone
they use to make us, laugh and cry

Fathers they were sons and brothers too
men of families, men too proud not to be

For our men I fear that in thee end,
we shall perish not ever knowing why!

Right There

When I am gone and you're all alone
I know there will be crying
you'll feel like your dying

But when it's all over and you have gone on
you'll know in your heart then
that I'm really right there.

So Much Pain

There's so much pain
I try hard to hold on
but, every time I reach out
There is nothing but, hurt and pain

A new beginning I once thought
but no not for me
alone again no matter what
always ending here

Thinking how I feel inside
crying all night long

in my mind I think I've won
but the battle has just begun
I wish I could, I wish you would
take away this awful pain

After the Loss

I find myself wondering, how I would make it
after the loss of my love one

Though when A life ends another begins
there is only one you, who has touched my heart
my life and many others

It's hard to imagine life without you here
If I can only see your smiling face
or the way you walk and talk
or even when you cry inside

I would imagine you're a person
that will never be forgotten
even after the loss

The Parents That I Adore

As a child I can only cry out,
for what I have grown to love
Your my parents the ones that I adore
though there are times it does not show
for you're the one's that I admire most

And in my darkest hours when times are low
I think of the parents that I adore.

Who have worked hard from day to day
perhaps more than I ever could

yet never giving up on me
a child without the knowledge
of what they know now

You're my parents, my guide, my everything
I thank God almighty you were there for me.

Close To You

There's something that brings me close to you
somewhere, where I don't care
I've held my ground then turned around
Clinging to the midnight air

Short from grace I can't escape
this love you set deep in place
somewhere deep, deep inside
somewhere where I don't care

Son

I never thought the son I bear
would grow to be so fair
from the tomb of my womb
comes this child that dared to care

You are on your way with a future ahead
so watch your back and don't despair
you're a child again in a world of fear

Cynthia

Thank you dear father for my faith in you
you have brought me a long way
with a long way to go

Though I have cross many paths
and climb many mountains
I still need you to guide me through

So thank you dear father
for the strength you have given me
I know I haven't lost anyone
I 'm regaining my soul

And dear Cynthia my darling
the love of our life
we love you, we miss you
now rest in peace

Love and Happiness

*Sharing your lives together as one
this is who we are
not just man and woman but one
as God had intended us to be.*

*At last the search for true love has ended
a man for a woman, a woman for a man
this day marks a new beginning now
facing the world head on*

*For as many years
as it has taken you to come together
your love shall intensify 10 times over.*

Sleepless Nights

Sometimes I lay awake at night
wondering if things will ever change

Long sleepless nights
my life seems consumed of work and no play

But yet I seem content at times
with this life I chose of sleepless nights

Blue Rose

This is not a blue rose because I am feeling blue.
This is a blue rose to inspire you

So that you will remember that in the mist of it all
That you are still the best

And when the sky is blue, you'll know that I'm thinking of you
and all that is within your reach.

Remember son, blue moments are small but
an accomplishment will last forever!

Moments

*There's nothing more I'd love to do
then cuddle up next to you
with your arms around me
and mine around you
embracing ever so close*

Black America

Yes! My skin is Dark, Mahogany perhaps
A beautiful rich dark skin
For African blood flows
Through my veins
But, then again so do yours
And Now I can not claim
Which was once mine to claim?
For I am a made
Of this land
I Am Black America

History

Give me something to remember
Give me something to be proud
Give me my dignity
Give me my soul
Give me something that I can hold
Give me my true history, waiting to be told

A Story to Tell

Tell me a story
Tell me of when we were once kings and queens
Tell me a story
Of the great ones who die knowing their names
Tell me a story of the children who ran free
Tell me a story of love and respect
Tell me a story of the way our fathers were
Tell me then teach me so I will know
Please tell me; please tell me, so I may be free too

Knowledge

I am starving for knowledge
Feed my soul with the knowledge of the old
Teach me the way of our past
Love me in the way of life once lived
Oh! Old one I am ready to learn
Teach me oh great one
I am yearning to learn
For my heart is burning with a desire to learn
Give me what you have learned
For I am starving for knowledge
I am ready to learn

Love of my life

Watching you and seeing you in my every thought
There was never a need to be near
For in my thoughts stood you
holding me until we were together again

I thought I must be dreaming to feel so alive
Not sure what to do with this strange kind of love
That seems to leave me not thinking
a care in the world
So I must be in love with the love of my life

For Now My Love

My love for you has made me turn, then run away.
A love that grows with each and every day.
You've changed my life my heart's no longer blue
But, when it aches it aches for you.
For now my love, I love you too
You have cared for me and I for you
So I'm here for now and now I'll stay
As our love grows stronger and stronger each day

Commitment

Marriage these words seem to haunt me now
It seems it has no real meaning
It seem to be such a waste
Why can't we be friends, or lovers

Why should we move on to be more committed?
When what we have is the best of us yet.
After all we are committed
Committed to being who we are

About the Author

Ms Carter enjoys the life of her suburban home in Gaines Township where she resides. She's a member of the American Legion and a future entrepreneur. She has two children Derek and Shawunia, two grandchildren onah and Juliana. Outside activities and hobbies include computers, web esign, community work and family. Ms Carter's first published poem Hear Me" which influenced to continue to write poetry and pursue the ublication of this book (Songs from the Heart).

About the Book

Songs from the Heart is a book of poetry based some of the things that he and her friends have experienced in life. It's sort of a non-fiction fictional tory about things people deal with every day such as death, love, and the eart breaks of life.

This book of poetry is something that lets her express how she views the world around her in her day to day life. There are many ways of expressing ourselves, poetry is her way to release lifes frustrations of what she feels we ll go through.